Lola

Tim McLaurin

DOWN HOME

Down Home Press, Asheboro, N.C.

ISBN 1-878086-62-6

Library of Congress Catalog Card Number
97-069229

Printed in the United States of America

Cover art by Gary Hawkins
Cover design by Tim Rickard
Book design by Beth Glover

Down Home Press
P.O. Box 4126
Asheboro, N.C. 27204

This book is dedicated to
Sandy Arnold

And even yet
sometimes I pause
and raise both arms
as if to weigh the measures of my life
—one hand calloused and full
—the other palm up and yearning

I would like to express my thanks to the following
people who contributed greatly to the
publication of this poem:
Donnalee Frega who encouraged these words from
the beginning; Erik Bledsoe, who is an excellent
editor; Beth Glover, whose talent for design is
matched by her eye for story; and Jerry Bledsoe, a
good drinking buddy,
a fellow fisherman, and my publisher.

Part One

The Serpent

God's curse upon the serpent is not the lack
of legs to walk upright.
His curse is eyes that cannot close.
No lids to hide, if only for a while,
the passing of an age and life.

Many people have gathered here in praise of
    a good man.
Two hundred strong they number,
men who have worked his fields, bought his
    grain,
repaired his combines and his teeth,
and hunted in bands the woodland and
    meadows.
Most admired him, a few despised him,
but everyone has come,
their children scrubbed clean and

their wives in tow bearing homages
of fried chicken and layer cakes.
John Wesley Stewert is dead,
a Southern farmer,
one less of an endangered breed.

What have I watched from the gnarled branch
of this great oak?
What have I not seen?
I wish now that I could close my view of
    a farm
surrounded by new houses built on half-acre
    lots,
blacken my sight in the clean light of morning
to the fact that now I count more cars on the
    roadway
than mourning doves cooing their sorrow from
    pine tops.

Twenty years I have digested my supper of
    young birds and squirrels,
the few eggs I snatched from his barn.
But I held my bargain.
"Snake," he said when our paths first
    crossed—
My length was less than that of his boot—
"Eat more mice than my hen eggs,

and we can share these fine acres.
Eat more eggs than mice,
and I will test the words of old women
    and see
whether a snake chopped into small pieces can
    draw together at sunset."

Today I am longer than five of his boots,
thicker than his lower arm,
muscle and fat gained from the barn mice—
the occasional egg.
I kept my bargain old man,
as you kept your word with this serpent
and with men and women gathered now to
    sing hymns and weep.

The air smells of earth turned
following a hard spring rain,
worms and grubs, the sweet roots of fescue
    grass.
This hole they have dug in the hilltop,
dark and warm and moist like the womb,
is now your mother.

Your mother's dress is bright with the colors
    of May,
and pleated with rolling fields and pasture,

forest, the lap of pond water against cattail
    rushes.
Three hundred acres,
upon my belly flutes I have wandered,
boundary to boundary, and hunted the
    field mice,
swallowed the young starling and blackbird,
and in the season between the going and
    coming of the frost,
rested only occasionally upon warm rocks.
The time of ice calls me,
as it called you.
I know each tree blazed by surveyor's ax,
each benchmark and fence line,
how your land slopes from the high, dry woods
east toward the fertile bottom soil beside
    the river.

If I had eyelids,
I would close them and in my mind
see you by the river
where the rocks stand like great turtles.
I would see you there with Lola,
happy with only a cane pole and can of
    fishing worms.

Man, from this high branch

I hold the bird's sight and I scout your land
    for you
these people who have gathered,
the scars of bulldozers that nudge your
    fence line.
Slowly the chosen six walk to the rear of
    the long, black car.
They will bear you these several yards
across the field to the earth.
David, your son,
Fenner, the hired man,
four others who have shared your liquor
    and your life.
They will plant you under dirt and flowers,
and a gray stone will proclaim you once lived.
I know that you have lived,
as I know that you are dead as I shall be too.

The face of your oldest, Julia,
says you are dead.
She will mourn you the proper forty days,
wear sack cloth and weep,
and only then count her birthrights.
She will count them.

Young Lola—
the touched one born from an aged womb—

will not count her birthrights.
She marks the days until you return.

If I had the bird's gift,
I would settle on her shoulder and preen
    her ear
and whisper that she will find you
where the river breeds with rocks,
your voice mingled with the song of flowing
    water.
What truths you can tell her
now that your soul is stretched
between stream and star.

But I am earthbound,
no wings, not even legs.
But I do possess, unwanted,
eyes that cannot close out a past remembered
and a time I fear is coming.

David

Fifty steps must I walk
and not show the strain of this load.
I must grip the polished brass knob
like I wished to grasp his hand.
I must step fifty paces, my back erect
and bear this weight.
Can there be a greater honor than a son carry
    his father to rest?
He carried me home from the field
the day the copperhead sank his fang in
    my leg,
lifted me from the board
where the nail pierced my shoe,
skewered between leather and flesh,
toted me from his shed
where he stored the grape wine
the night my legs refused my call.

I will carry him, one foot before the last,
and be careful my shoe does not slip into the
    machine-dug hole.
I should have dug it with my hands,
molded clay and sand so that his head
would rest in a cradle not sculpted by
    cold steel.
What else should I have done
had I known that fathers really die,
what words might I have spoken from
    my heart?
If God would let me,
I would lift him now from this coffin
and race around the world against the sun,
one thousand laps
to turn back the clock one-thousand days,
if in that span returned to us
we would talk
instead of hiding our words in thoughts
buried for lack of time and courage
to speak.

If I could tell him my regrets,
the words would speak of chores undone,
the calf unfed, the grass uncut,
the weed not pulled

when that labor was trusted to me.
Too often I rested in the shade
when his figure was a mark against
        distant trees.
In a box I hid thoughts, pictures, and poems
we could not speak of or share.
I have sinned,
but not in trespass, theft, or lies,
but in my arms that hung by my sides
and did not hold.

Hold to this box, arms; walk steady, feet;
eyes, look not left or right
but only upon the place where the earth is torn.
It is his bed, his rest.
I will plant his blanket in clover and fescue,
his pillow will be fat, marbled clay,
and his stone shall read
here sleeps in eternal peace
a good man I barely knew.

Julia

I feel their stares
upon the nape of my neck.
I see the women's sideward glances,
the men's eyes that dart to me and turn.
I suppose as the elder child,
I am expected to fall prostrate
across the path of these pallbearers,
hold tight to my brother's leg and beg him
not to bear to earth the remains of our father.
Behind this black veil,
my eyes should weep the tears of a first-born,
my breath short and sour
with the taste of death.
I might try and cover his mouth
with my own and blow my soul
into his lungs that he would rise
and walk these fields again.

I would,
if such strain would raise him from the dead,
but that action would prove futile
as fishing upon sand.
He did not raise me
to spend myself on what is already damned.
Did I not know this man,
his dreams and wishes and demands of me?
"Julia," he would say,
"one cannot count the grains of sand,
nor should she waste time trying,
but she can count the coins in her purse,
the days in a week, in a year, and wager them
    against
the time already lost from our lives.
Don't tarry."

Have I tarried father?
Speak to me now with your ghost tongue,
and I will hear you on the wind if I have
    tarried.
I will hear your complaint as thunder
in the west sky.
I count my obedience in both hands,
one calloused and full,

one soft as dove down, palm-up and
yearning.

Possessions accumulated in thirty-four years:
one swept house paid for on shaded land,
and money saved in three banks.
I do not answer the orders of any man.
No wedding band to weigh my finger,
I command my own mop and broom.
The other hand shows only the stain of ink
from turning the picture pages in magazines.
It has not labored under the countless chores
of rearing my own children,
the scars of loving them.
This hand is flawless and fragrant and fragile
and empty.

But my heart is not fragile,
it lies within my chest like a lump of iron,
no threat of fracture.
"Take care of her," he said.
Not "Take care of yourself."
"Take care of her, take care of her,"
The imperfect one,
Lola.

I don't rage against the visit of death.

Death is the mark of time,
and time rules us.
Bear him to the earth, brother.
I have loved him as only this daughter can love
    her father,
and though my tears are dry,
and my heart cannot tremble,
he is the anvil and the hammer and fire,
and I will mourn him in my own way.

Neighbors smile at me,
touch my hand and say they are sorry.
I too am sorry, but my grief spans years
instead of these few days.
Instead of sobbing, I wish I could shout,
"Father, if I had known you
as my brother knew you,
as you knew the rolls and forest of your land,
as Lola knew you and knows now
the words to simple lullabies."
Then I might now feel rivers upon my cheeks
and fall prostrate like a woman whose heart
is soft and yearning
as her hand never filled.

Lola

Daddy is in a box, and he is sleeping,
and when he wakes we will eat ice cream.
This party is so full of people.
It must be my birthday again.
I am many,
all my fingers and four rocks.
Maybe they have brought me presents,
and we will all eat cake and ice cream,
and float balloons above the treetops.

A woman was crying, and I touched her hand
    and asked why.
Her face made my tears drip too—
sad on this day with sunshine and clouds
and a party?
She smiled and said, "Child."
Maybe she wishes for her own party.

I will share it all,
this fine day,
sun and pretty clouds,
the ice cream.
I hope it is peach.

Do you like my dress?
I love how it swishes
so full on my legs
like the wind before the rain falls.
My dress is new.
Do you like my bonnet?
The flowers on it aren't real, but they look real,
and when I close my eyes I can smell them
like the daffodils that grow by the river
where Daddy takes me.
Do you like my new shoes,
all shiny and black like my dress,
like storm clouds?
I like blue better.
They have all dressed up for the party
like Sunday,
even Mr. Fenner, my buddy who feeds
    the cows
and cuts the corn.
He is pretty in his white shirt and tie.

I will give him two helpings of cake and
ice cream.
His face is so grim.
Maybe my daddy's bed is heavy.
Or maybe he got stung by a bee.
I will mix baking soda and water to stop
    the hurt,
and if that does not make him smile,
I will go to Julia.
Julia always knows what to do.

Fenner

Already I feel a storm brewing.
The dark clouds have covered Julia's face,
and in David's white knuckles
lightning flashes.
Lola is talking, and in her sweet voice
I hear the splatter of rain.

Man, you died on me,
and I always thought I would be the one
carried home from the field.
Friend,
you paid me fair wages.
We shared the same bottle of bourbon and
traded stories men tell.
Twenty years I have worked your farm,
birthed the calves,
cut grain and corn and mended fences,

and ate from the same meal—
fried corn bread and butterbeans
cooked with ham meat,
sweet tea in a Mason jar.
Did that ham meat bust your heart?
Was it finally the fried chicken and yeast rolls
filled with butter?
The meals were good, eaten on tractor seats,
sometimes our table drawn from a stump,
or in the shade of the willows beside the river
where the rocks lay.
I hurt to think of the river meadow,
but if there is a heaven,
yours is there beside that flowing water.
I could easier count the stars
than remember all the times we wet hooks
     there,
or wet our wicks with the Dawson sisters,
or finished off a quart of Jim Beam
and talked
of how a man raises children without a woman.

I don't think evil can exist beside that water,
     no sin.
Those banks are balanced
between heaven and hell

in a corner where neither God nor Satan
    visits,
and if what a man feels there in his heart
    is just,
he holds the same in his hands.
But now clouds are stirring,
and I fear Julia's dark veil
is brighter than her heart.
And David, little soldier, scholar man,
can only reason through his books.
I already worry for dear, sweet,
Lola.

I would have cut off my ears
rather than hear your shout in the field,
where you slumped on the combine.
I would have ripped out my eyes so I didn't
see you fall
and I come running,
if I had known your last request.
But like a blaze of lightning,
my brain is seared.
I would trade my oath to you now
for my belly filled with snakes,
because a storm is brewing,
and not in the clouds.

Part Two

The Serpent

I see Stewert's resting spot atop the far hill,
still brilliant with color like the eye of Earth,
the life sap of cut flowers not leached after
    three days.
I have witnessed strange events.
The cows gather each evening in a ring
    around the hill
and low and bellow in chorus;
the hogs have stopped eating
and turn up their snouts even at corn.
The birds came in flocks on the twilight
    after his planting
and adorned the single oak above his
    gravesite,
robins, starlings, bluebirds, and crows—
they do not usually gather—

but in the hundreds weighed the branches
    and sang,
and as if on cue took wing
and circled round and wide and left.

I have felt you through my belly scales,
    man,
as I felt the offshoots of the young bull who
    died of bloat,
the patter of young goats birthday stillborn.
The Mrs. when she died in birth
brushed my back like a stroke of wind.
You are one with the wind now, the rain,
your atoms diffused with those
of clay and air.
I feel you as the fledgling bird shall feel
    my slither
on the day of my rest
and then no longer need fear me.

This branch is limber and sways me gently,
and I wish I could close my eyes and sleep
not be witness
to battle plans.
Tell me a battle is not brewing,
and I will swear I do not like the robin's egg.
The man has brought his skin of papers,

as he did on days when land was bought,
the birth of children and the death of Mrs.
He sits with Julia, David, and the
    helping man
in a ring of garden chairs in shade.
They sip iced tea through straws.
Lola plays in the dust with a doll
minus eyes, one arm and clothes.
She loves it.
Julia bites her straw
until its crook is like a lightning bolt.
David sits straight and tall,
unbending,
as if he fears his father's voice through
    the soil.
The helping man, Fenner,
has nothing to harness his hands and they
    wrestle
like young boys upon his lap.

I should leave from here,
but this branch is slender and my flight
might prompt Julia to fetch the rifle,
she the eagle eye.
I have no lids to hide behind,
so I must read this man's lips
and learn the battle lines of this war.

These words I fear to repeat.

"I have gathered you good people
to recall the last thoughts and will
of the Christian man, John Wesley Stewert,
may he rest in peace.
Not a better man has breathed air
or walked a fairer piece of land
than his acreage of hardwoods and hills,
the fertile belly land of corn fields
and wheat.
The land rolls like a serpent's back
and slopes gently to the delta soil of river
     land.
This land he loved, as you he loved
and left you in deed
his land and his soul—hear his words.

'Julia and David, stand
and turn the east to west
and scope your land.
Spin like a whirlwind and the colors
that flash before your eyes you own.
Fire the rifle at the moon,
and the bullet will fall to earth and bury
in soil of your deed,
shout,

and the echo that returns to your ear
rebounds from trees and hills you now
    possess.
I have willed you equal the farm,
what pastures and woodlands and grain bins
to own jointly and fashion
between brother and sister
what testament of partnership and custody
suits you.

I ask that Lola
live within your domain,
that you love and keep her
as I and you have kept her these years,
and that the decisions of her life
shall now be yours.

Stand up, Fenner,
and hold your chin high as a man who owns
    land.
We were like brothers.
You will enter no more a house of tenancy
or hoe your beans and corn on land
owned by another, for I will
that the twelve acres and the house where
    you abide
shall be your own in name and law,

where you might dwell your days
under song of locust and tree frog
the duet of mourning doves,
and labor as you have worked these years
in the same fields you and I toiled.
May the partnership with my son and
    daughter
please you and them and feed you 'til
old age delivers your own rest.

As for Lola.
What can I leave to a woman-child
that desires only to hold the moon and stars
in her palm
and blow them like dandelion?
What can land and silos mean to one
who cannot count her own fingers
but knows every cow by name and kin?
I leave to her the river meadow,
that scant two-acre western corner
where the land is joined to water.
There we fished and chased the minnow,
caught the leopard frog and bothered the
    crayfish,
picnicked on the sandbar
in the shade of willows.
This land is fallow but to one like Lola

who talks back to the babble of water
and to the dragonfly.
She sees diamonds on the river's surface,
every colored rock an emerald,
each fleck of mica as hammered gold.
These treasures are only as real
as her imagination, and her mind
charts land not seen by pioneers.
Child may you find pleasure and fortune
with these jewels,
may they fill your heart as you have filled
  mine.
I will speak to you on summer evenings
in the quiet lap of water.
Hear my stories in the frog's song,
my face reflected in the smooth, deep pools
beneath the willow's shade.'"

I now doze on this tree limb, warm in
  noon sun,
the drone of June bugs, the yelp of
  the hound.
The air vibrates with the sound of a distant
  hammer
where Fenner has gone to mend fences.
The man with the skin bag took no coins.
He said his fee was paid in memories.

What memories have David and Julia
carried from this shade tree?
I see them in the distance,
walking different fields,
every stride carrying them further from
    each other
in space and mind.

They are landowners.
I wonder if I should fare as well
if I were to cross their paths
as did I with their father?
Does a bargain struck with him bind
unto his children?
I must tread well, but now I will rest
for the June bug sings of sleep and the sun
    is warm,
and this branch sways slowly with the wind.

David

Am I a rich man?
Am I now a man at last, at thirty years
    of age?
It is time.
I have stood too long in my father's shadow.
This beautiful slice of land,
my father bought with his tears and sweat,
forest cleared to farm land,
and with the passing of his breath it is mine.
So easy.

But I have paid.
Count my earned degrees.
A rank of sergeant at the Sewanee Institute
    for Boys,
three seasons from the years of my life
playing soldier and marching to drums.

I excelled.
A double degree in agriculture and
    economics
from the State University where I graduated
    with honors.
I paid the price, Father, as you asked,
and now I know how best to grow
corn, wheat, and barley,
breed registered cows and raise pigs to
    market,
but only in theory and on paper.
I have not sweated much or bled.

I remember your blood,
the day you came home from the back acres
where you and Fenner were clearing land,
your thumb laid against your palm
like some pink, tender vegetable,
cut clean through the bone with a bush ax.
You packed it in ice and ordered the doctor
to sew it back on,
walked nights, cursed and raved
while the thumb turned green, then black,
    ran pus,
and finally healed.

In my palm I scoop an orb of wet soil.

Granular. I must get my probe and have
    samples sent
to be tested in the lab.
Might need more phosphate or potash,
maybe a little sodium.
Father,
I remember how you would smell the dirt
    and taste it,
your senses more acute and trained
than the machines in laboratories.
Are worms present and grubs?
Does the soil clot or crumble?
The county man was never called
    or needed
to grow corn the height of a basketball goal
and melons as big as young hogs.

See the cows grazing fescue.
They are birthing.
I have marked in journals the dates
of each heifer's first heat, blood lines,
the sons and daughters.
Father, you kept no books,
only reams in your head of facts and figures
they do not teach in school.
I must book the county man
for next year's breeding season.

With his stainless steel rod he can fertilize
    more cows
in one day
than the bull's heart could stand in a week.
Yet you stayed with him,
led him on ring and tether to the bridal lot
where the heifer stood waiting,
her vagina blinking.

How did you know from the cow's udder,
the way she stood, walked, or lowed
what hour she would deliver?
I have seen you with your rope and soapy
    water
pull the calf's head straight and guide him
between the narrow pelvic bones of his
    mother,
clean the mucus from his nose
and blow air into his nostrils until he stood
on wobbly legs.
I have the phone number of a veterinarian
who will come even in late-night hours
with his shiny, sterile tools.
We roomed together at school.
I keep his number handy.

Without water, neither seed

nor semen can exist.
"Trust not in God for the rain,
but dig wells," you said.
Three ponds I count, the slow slope
of the field to the river,
and if all that fails we have the artesian
sunk two-hundred feet through limestone.
The heat of an atom bomb could not
    vaporize
that clear, primal water.
I recall the day the engineer came
with his Sonar and graphs and maps.
They broke diamond bits in three locations
trying to bore through dry rock
before you brought out the water witch,
and walked back and forth across the land
'til that wood twisted in your hand,
so determined to point to earth
that bark shredded, your skin burned.
"Dig here," you told the engineer,
and he bet you the price of that drilling
that your spot would yield no better,
and at one-hundred-ninety feet the earth
    shook
and water sprayed skyward clear as
    diamonds.

None of this you learned in books.
I know books,
but I do not know what length to snap the
    willow branch
so that it turns and burns against my palms,
or the feel of the calf's wet head
still inside his mother.
Ask me to taste dirt, and I will say
it tastes only of clay and worms.
I have not sweated in this dust,
or bled in it.
I watched the labor of hired men
from tractor seats and truck windows.
You said, "It is best so;
bend the pages of books instead of your
    back."
I read pages while you read the cow's udder,
and paid your price to inherit this land.

But not the river crossing,
those rocks that split the water
and channel the smooth flow into current.
Those banks were always my favorite,
far beyond grain fields and pastures filled
    with cows.
In the shade of those willows I wished
for what Lola has lived.

I did not tell you, Father,
of the ten-point buck I shot there,
the day I took the rifle when you said
I was too young to hunt.
Call it an accident or the will of God
that a boy with a weapon as long as myself
could stand by the water
and watch a wild animal come to drink
    and die.
So quietly he moved,
sniffing the air and rolling his tongue,
he swung his great antlers and searched,
while I waited in the shadows.
I recall the folds of skin that hung from
    his neck,
his ears pitched forward and tuned
to the sound of quick water, the wren's song.
I feared he would hear me breathe.
He came to the river's edge,
passed me in the tangle of willow and reeds,
lowered his head and drank.
A bluejay cried as I lifted that big gun
    and aimed.
I do not recall pulling the trigger,
but I felt the jolt and heard the roar of
    the powder

wash over bird songs and rippling water,
and stagger that buck sideways.
He leapt, buckled, and died in seconds
in the shallows.
I let him float away on the current,
no knife on my belt to carry home his
      gushing heart,
no courage to tell you, Father,
I had taken your gun.
His body swung in wide circles,
the blood diffusing in red fingers,
his eye open and shiny and reflecting
the lights of heaven.
I have killed no more deer.

I first spilled my seed in the secret of that
      willow shade
where neither God nor buck could see me,
leering at a magazine taken from your high
      bedroom shelf,
and without knowing why
pulling at that part of me
until I cried out and sprayed my fluid,
pumped like the buck's pierced heart
      spilled blood,
and I felt sudden shame at my wound.

A tall poplar tree
grows by the water,
unique among the willows and pines,
some wayward seed carried to plant by
    high water.
Many hours I sat in her branches,
above even song birds,
where the wind sways the trunk and
trembles leaves
like many soft hands.
What did I observe from there?
Crows nestled in a nearby pine in a great
    bowl of needles
who cawed out to me not to try and fly
    without wings.
The large snake I spied one day resting
on a lower branch,
fat from young birds, as thick as a limb.
Hours I waited, afraid,
until he unfurled and crawled down
    the trunk
in crooks, like slow lightning.
Foxes, racoons came to drink, the widowed
    doe and fawn,
mallard ducks that swooped in to rest
and flung themselves skyward
at the report of my clapped hands.

The two plump women,
I saw them too,
the day you and Fenner brought them
to the river,
laughing,
and drinking whiskey from a bottle.
They danced round and round like
    well-fed elves.
I saw you take them into the water, pink
    and naked,
and wash and rub and splash and run
    in circles
and go in pairs to the willow shade
where I was glad I could not see.

A place of secrets,
two scant acres that touch water,
wasteland for all but memories.
Why do I linger in my mind at those rocks
when beneath my feet are three-hundred
    acres?
I do not know.

I do know I would trade all this
for what Lola possesses,
that smile on her face, her words so simple.

She holds in her hands and mind all that is
    treasured.
I have watched from the blueberry bushes
times you took her fishing,
using reed pole, corks, and worms;
she squealed when she snatched tiny bream
    and perch,
wiggling,
from that sparkling water.
The day she snagged the catfish,
ten pounds of flapping tail, spine erect,
a load for any frying pan,
she threw him back,
cheering.

I have watched you two march away from
    the house,
paper-sack lunches in hand,
Lola with her butterfly net,
highstepping,
as if off to snare dragons.
From my hiding spot, Father, I saw
    your smile,
chuckle, fits of laughter,
Lola's dance, her race behind butterflies
    and moths,
her squeals over the tadpole you lifted

from between two mossy stones.
I saw, too, the day she stepped into trouble
in the quiet, deep pool,
go under and only her face reappear.
She did not scream as you came for her,
not shedding windbreaker or boots,
you lifted her with arms that easily tote
two bales of hay and carried her
to the dry sand,
combed her hair with your fingers
and said, "Little one"
over and over like the dove's coo.

I would trade all these fertile acres
for what we might have shared—
your hand on my shoulder and your blessing
when I drew bead on the buck's heart.
You standing at my shoulder,
instructing how to cut his throat,
and watching me from my cupped palm
drink his salty blood,
his tenderloin anointing the next
    Thanksgiving table.
The meaning of one's seed
I learned from boars and bulls.
I wish you had told me of men and women,
rather than leaving me to see

shaded images of pink, plump women
who squeal naked in the water.
I have felt your occasional hand
on my shoulder in passing,
seen your face in the crowd
when I walked across the graduation stage,
where I was handed a paper that claims
I know how to sow my harvest of grain,
    corn, and cows.
Another piece of paper says I now possess
three-hundred acres of land.

Julia

Three-hundred acres of land I own,
decreed by will and law.
Aren't they truly mine by squatter's rights?
I turn in a circle and know every path and
    truck rut,
where the crow nests in the pine thicket,
the quail's chamber in the bramble
along the field's edge.
I have been tied to this land
by an umbilical cord,
and that rope is short and does not stretch
except between land boundaries.
It tightened every step I walked to
    the mailbox,
carried me home from school on fleet foot
    each afternoon,
and hummed like a tight guitar string

every time I ventured so far as to shop for
food and soap and linen.

I must have pleased you, Father,
to leave me equal in land
and worth by the labor of my hands
what my brother earned on paper.
What is my title besides "lonely"—
Land baroness, spinster, independent
    woman?
My degree is held in shades of mood.
I will plow this wheat and corn under
and plant these fields in iris and red poppy,
and clover with pink blossoms
ungrazed by goats and cows.

My dowry will be the frock of nature,
and not the sight of a man's back
as he walks in morning light to castrate
    young bulls,
mend fences and cut corn.
I will weave a shawl of these flowers
and hold it over my head and twirl
and say "I am the Baroness of Blossoms,
a rose yet unfurled."

Lola is a flower,

her mind like the ancient lotus
frozen in time and bloom,
fragrant and sweet to the eye and ear.
Her blossom will never truly unfold,
and yet it will never wilt.
She could walk my field of iris
and the stalks would bow a path,
and no one who looked would see my crop
    of colors,
except Lola.

This land has a heart,
and now Lola owns that heart,
as she has always owned the hearts
of my Father and Fenner,
and the hearts of wild rabbits and birds.
I despise that meadow beside the water,
the glint of sunshine on current
where leaves and twigs float like tiny
    freighters
on slow journeys to foreign ports.
I despise the dance of small bream and perch
snagged on Lola's fishing line,
their rainbow flash
fried brown in the oil of my cooking pan.
I despise picnic baskets I packed

with ham biscuits and slices of
    sweet potato pie,
and Mason jars of iced tea with lemon
I was not asked to share.
I despise stories of the beaver and the
    mallard ducklings,
and the spotted fawn,
the lies of elves and nymphs
peeping from the willow shade.
I despise those tales and memories,
second hand from Lola's lips.
They might have been my own.

But I am land-rich and have money,
and lay claim to Baroness of Blossoms.
"Till under the corn and fescue and sell the
    bull," I declare.
This land's heart I do not possess,
and I have not need
for what I never owned.

Fenner

Ring out ol' hammer,
drive this nail deep into the cypress post
so that I can mend this fence
and separate the cows from sweet corn.
I wish this one-pound bell I ring
would drown the voice inside my head,
and separate me from my thoughts.

Landowner, I now possess
a tie to this earth and am no longer free
as the robin, the rabbit and the fat, rat snake.
A man's words simply written on paper
and I own a portion of this earth.
Should I praise him?
John Stewert, we were like brothers,
and I heard your last words.
They ring even now like this hammer,

and threaten to split my skull
from ear to ear.
My brain crawls with worms.

Still, I heard your last words,
bent with my ears so close
I smelled the watermelon we had just split
and eaten with our hands.
I wish I had just pledged my loyalty
and were not saddled now with land.
Without it I might carry out my deed if
    called,
and then wander the earth in torn clothes,
rub my face with dust and eat clay
and swear I am the crazy man.
You have given me a home,
a tap root that ties my soul to bedrock.
Already I know I must oil that squeal
in the front door and add lumber
where the porch roof sags,
and live out my days in fear of my promise.

Ring out ol' hammer,
and carry like dynamite from the river rocks
to the highest hill on this land,
deliver my voice to Julia and David,

and demand that fences always need
    mending
on three-hundred acres of land,
undivided.
Knowing my oath,
I would rather suck the river into my lungs
and spew rain storms and winds
with my last breath.

Great God Almighty, am I caretaker?

Lola

I'm not supposed to come to the river.
Julia would be mad.
But she walked away so fast,
like Mr. Fenner and David
when the man finished reading the paper.
It frightened me.
Julia says maybe one day I will learn
    to read,
but I don't want to if it makes people frown
and hurry from one another.

The man patted my shoulder and said
the river and the rocks
where Daddy takes me fishing
are mine, and only mine.
I started to laugh.
The river cannot belong only to me.

It belongs to the fishes
and the turtles and the big green frogs.
It belongs to the cows
that come here to drink,
and to the goats and to the white water birds
that sometimes fly in.
It belongs to Mr. Fenner and to David
    and Julia,
although David and Julia never take me
    here.
I will not be greedy.

When I lean from this rock and dip my hand
I feel the water flowing.
Daddy told me no one can own a river
because it slides away
and what is here tomorrow is a new piece
    of water.
So I can pretend it's mine
but this water I splash,
yesterday belonged to another little girl
and a frog and cow and fish,
and maybe even an older sister who likes
    picnics.

I will share this river.
When Daddy wakes up I will ask him

to tear up the paper that says the river
    is mine.
He knows better anyway.
No one can own a tree or river
or a rock or a flower or a cloud.
They are there for us to look at and touch
    and smell
and make us smile.

I better go now.
Julia will be mad.
I hear Mr. Fenner with his hammer,
and maybe he will let me help him hit
    the nails.
Hear me, big green frog,
Mr. White Bird who stands on one leg,
I will pretend this piece of river is mine,
but don't ever be afraid because
I know it is forever really ours.

Part Three

The Serpent

Two skins I have shed this season,
twice watched the full moon rise through
    tree boughs.
The wreaths are gone from the hilltop,
and the grass grows thick upon the old
    man's bed.
Cows low in the evening and the kid goats
frolic and twist.
The locusts ring in verse with frogs and
    crickets,
and the sun settles slowly in the red, western
    sky.
Yet, I feel winter is upon me,
an ache in my bones that will not heal
and a chill in these three-hundred acres
that goes beyond falling, yellowed leaves
to a depth buried under many feet of snow.

The hay has not been cut and stored in
    the barns;
the fescue has grown past a man's knee.
Corn was only planted in half the fields;
the weeds thrive better than the grain.
Twice the long trailer has carried calves to
    market,
not fattened, but snatched from their
    mothers.
The bull has remained tethered in his pen.
Why hasn't the pumpkin field been tilled?
Already green vines should twist from
    the soil
like quarreling brothers.
Has David, possibly the hired man too,
forgotten that collards and turnips
should already be set
so they will cure in the first nips of frost?

Twice the man who totes the bag of skin
has sat under the tree with Julia and David.
I see pain in his face,
his words spew
like water from a deep well pumped.
The hired man spends his days mending
    fences.

His hammer rings like a tireless bird,
as if he hopes to contain
inside the wire a life and land
that seems destined to unbind and unfurl,
scattered,
like the dandelion's seed.
The child wanders the pasture,
still weaving her clover bracelets
and talking to herself.
She often sits beside the old man's grave,
curling grass around her finger
as she used to twist his hair.

Hurry bright sun to a high point
in this cloudless sky and warm my old
    bones.
I fear this chill is the first nod
of the sleep of age.

Lola

Wake up, Daddy.
Julia tells me you are only sleeping,
so tired from working in the field.
Wake up and I will give you this necklace
of clover blossoms and wild roses,
and kiss you on the cheek.
We will pack a picnic
and go and fish in the river.
Julia says you are only sleeping,
and the sun is warm and I
have not held your hand
for so long now.

Fenner does not talk to me, Daddy.
He works with his hammer
and stares at the grass or the sky.
We have always been pals,

and now he will not play with me.
I asked him how long you needed your
    sleep,
and he mumbled and looked away
and banged louder with his hammer,
Daddy,
the pumpkin patch has not been planted yet.
Remember how you always let me plant one
    seed
that was my very own, and we watched it
    grow
and then from the biggest pumpkin we
carved funny faces.
The calves are gone.
Their mothers run the pasture
and try to call them home.
I have heard David talk of selling the baby
    goats.
I cried to Julia, and she said
hush,
your father is sleeping, and you will wake
him.

Wake up, Daddy.
I don't care what Julia says.
I have made you bracelets.
I will be good and not cry

even if I step on a bee.
We will hold hands and walk the field
and plan when we will plant pumpkins,
and fish the still water beside the rocks.
You should not sleep so long.
Mr. Fenner told me a secret.
He has seen your face at the river
smiling up from where
in your dreams you swim with water bugs.

David

This shade is cool
and this chair more padded
than a tractor's seat.
I could sit here for another hour and read
good books and sip vodka mixed with
    seltzer and lime.
But I hear the hammer ringing.
Fenner waits for my command
and bides his time mending fences
as if history is bound to future years
through cypress post, barbed wire,
and nails.

I have let the corn grow thick with
    cockleburs;
the fescue is knee high.

I have grown a bumper crop in grass and
    weeds,
yet my shame is not real.
Father, if your spirit listens,
I have toiled in books and dirtied my hands
with ink stains, my fingers calloused
from typewriter keys,
and I can tell you all there is to know
of planting corn
and never need once to touch the kernel.
Am I to be ashamed for only following your
    wishes
that I be a learned man,
and call the corn flower a stamen,
the bull's swinging balls his testicles?
You listened to the beckon of the heifer's
    low,
the silent scrape of young wheat bursting
to day's light,
and I hear now the rustling call
of notebook pages, a textbook,
the scrape of chalk against a college
    blackboard.
I can pass on to hundreds
the knowledge you struggled to teach me
and let that boy who hears your same call of
    nature

be the one to till the soil.

Fenner, ring your bell and call me,
but fences close as much out
as they encircle.
I have spoken with Julia and know
only the iceberg's crest
of her dreams and problems,
but they open and close and are dark and
    shining
as the purple morning glory.
We speak of selling land.
Fenner, you are growing old
and justified is your inheritance of acreage
    and home.
May your hair grow white there as surely
    and quietly
as snow falls.
Cease to hammer me into the fields,
for I have been heated and cast
from another urn.
Let the man who hungers for the feel of
    earth
crumbling through his hands
possess the land,
and I shall teach his children
how they can feed a hundred hungry men,

and maybe in this balance
a day will come
when a kernel of corn
grows as tall and heavy with fruit
as a sweetgum tree.
I dream, but they are dreams as real
as the shine I saw in my father's eyes
when he pulled the newborn calf,
dried her,
and held her first to nuzzle
that rich, first mother's milk.

Do not berate me, Fenner,
for I do not shy from the fear of working
    with my hands,
but is not a son's first duty
to fulfill his father's command?
Father, hear me.
Do I speak wrong with thoughts of walking
from this land?
If I am wrong, talk to me in thunder,
rumble your displeasure between the clouds
and I will re-examine my stature
as a man.

I hear summer locust,
and the tinkling of ice cubes in my glass,

and Fenner's ceaseless hammer.

Hush, man.

Julia

Even now from this window
from where I sop and clean the dinner dishes
I see her,
Lola.
She sits as the brightest spot upon the
     hilltop,
weaves her flowers and talks to him
of childish things. Does she think his reply
will channel through quartz sand
and chips of feldspar
and buzz like a radio in her ear?

I see Lola always.
If not etched in color against my retina,
I know her path in memory,
where she places every bare foot,
stoops to pick the daffodil

and twirls round and round across the lawn
like God's favorite whirlwind.
She would call me mother,
had not her mind been formed as gentle
and simple, as the orphaned lamb
who frolics and follows first
the one who rubs her muzzle.
Fourteen years I have replaced her mother.
I was the one who changed her diapers,
and placed the fake teat in her mouth,
praised her crayon scratch,
bathed her, dressed her,
and eased the fear of her first menstrual
    blood.

My price? I will tell you.
A world known through *National
    Geographic*,
and men courted and loved and caressed
in *Cosmopolitan*.
I hid those pages beneath my mattress.
Father, I will hear no scolding,
my ears not tuned for the bedrock
where dead men sleep.
You lead Lola even now.
The lamb
will graze your grass blanket and wait

for the one who fed her cubes of praise
from his mouth and palms.

At night I dream of palm trees in Maui,
of the squat stand of the Eiffel Tower,
and a building in Rome where gods lived.
I look beyond poor Cuban migrant workers,
and see well-muscled men in fishing boats
in Greece.
They beckon with white teeth and bottles of
    Retzina.

In mind and dreams I walked circles
around this world.
On sleepless nights
when Lola's breath whistled through the
    yoke of croup,
fever and flu,
I held her and rocked her,
while my brother, and you, Father,
slept,
your wind as steady as the wall clock
that slowly ticked away the years.

Baroness, I am now titled,
not of the corn crop and gleamed wheat,
but of flowers.

If for once my wishes are granted.
I will draw inward these distant fields and
    encircle them
with stones from the river,
and plant beds of tulip and rose and
    snapdragon,
fields of yellow, red, and white.
Let the stalks grow uncultivated and wild
like the stirrings in my heart,
while I wander this globe for years.
When I grow weary and return home,
these colors will beckon to me like the
    homing glow
of a light house.

Brother,
tilt your glass and read
in the mottled sweetgum shade
the minds of men who dirty not their hands.
That is the farm you know,
these fields as alien to you,
as fishing men in Greece to me.
We will find no quarrel.

Fenner,
slam your hammer
and warn of wavering from olden ways.

Your days as a farm hand are numbered.
What you have been given was fairly earned,
but you can park the grain thresher,
sell the bottom plow and manure spreader,
and learn to plant bulbs
and root weeds from flower beds.

Lola,
puppy-child, lamb that follows the sugared
    palm.
I have in mind for you a place
where they always sing lullabies
and speak kind words,
where golden fish swim circles in glass
    ponds,
and you can hold a bamboo pole
and close your eyes and believe
you sit beside him at the river.

Do not hate me, Father, if you read my mind
beneath your cover of fescue and quartz
    sand.
The dead must not fault the living
for desiring only to draw
a deeper breath.

Fenner

I have ceased my hammering.
I cannot mend fences
that are steadily trampled down.
Instead I walk like a specter along the
    far ridge,
a man whose time has passed,
my pockets stuffed with ears of corn
unshucked and bursting on the cob.
I wade a sea of grass that should have twice
been bound in bales with wire.
The field mouse must laugh
from his deep straw tunnel,
safe from the rat snake and the hawk's eye.
He will not laugh when his name is
    city mouse.

They have planted flags

across the field and pasture,
and cut and marked the land
into parcels like loaves of bread.
The hungry have gathered,
men who walk these lines with slobber
    gleaming
on their tongues.
They point and gesture and choose.
In their eyes I see mirrors that reflect
houses, stores, a parking lot.
The lawyer walks at their heels,
and is mournful like a hound baying at
    the moon.
No happier than I,
but still he walks and nods and collects
    papers
that are sealed with names
that might as well be blood.

Trucks with trailers come and go,
the cows, goats, and hogs herded like Noah
filling the Ark
before the storm,
calves torn from lowing mothers,
the kid goats bound within iron bars.
The favored brood sow slobbered and bit
    only air

and will be hung to age and cure
before the morning.
The old bull will see no more pastures of
   virgin heifers.
He plodded at the end of his chain,
head down, and snatched a last tuft of
   clover,
was loaded and carried from the land of
   his years.

Julia and David sit in the shade of the
sweetgum,
gesture and point like the wind vane
atop the barn,
between moods that flash like seasons
of rain, famine and sunshine.

David has his books,
they multiply like seed corn,
and in his hands they wield like swords.
He is king of the garden chair.

Julia's eyes travel further than a rifle bullet,
and I suspect she sees far beyond the men
who prowl and sniff and scratch the fields.
She has brought in rocks,
truck loads dumped in heaps inside

the path of flags.
Maybe she hopes to build a stone wall
and live within a castle as gray and cold
as the vision in her eyes.

Lola spends her day sitting
beside her father's grave.
She strings her flowers and sings to him.
Yesterday I heard her scold him.
"Get up," she said. "The animals are
     leaving."

Fortunately, she does not understand
how much of the world and life she has
     known
is in flight.
Her own grave chariot must arrive.
I hear the wheels like distant cannon,
and in the clouds I see smoke and dust
of a multitude beginning to walk
away from the life they knew.
If I were a younger man,
I would lift her in my arms and run
     from here.
But I am old, and what I have seen
     these weeks
has broken me.

Part Four

The Serpent

What is in the moon's face this strange
    night?
The leaves tremble.
The few remaining cows low
and the last sow walks circles round and
    round her pen.
I see light on the hillside where the old man
    rests,
but it is not a grass fire or lightning or torch,
but more akin to fireflies gathered
in the tens of thousands.
The light pulses and shimmers,
and grows brighter and larger,
like the heartbeat of an awakened man.

I tremble with the leaves
and feel winter's grind in my bones,

and know with my spirit
linked through millenniums to the Garden,
that what is wronged will be righted come
    sunrise.
I should hold with my belly scales to the
    rough bark
and wind myself in tight coils
and sleep until this great light passes,
but I have lived in oath with the old man
    and realize
what was mine and his
will soon be owned by lesser kin.
If I were the giant anaconda
I would consume this acreage,
every kid goat and fowl and piglet left,
so they might expire on land that is loved
and not be slain by the butcher's knife.
I would lie in wait in ditches and streams
and devour any man who envisions
    cornfields and grass
plowed under and paved.
I might even consume Lola,
so that one so innocent and trusting
would not have to see the bull carried to
    the blade.

But, I am not the anaconda,

the mere terror of song birds and field mice,
the occasional snatched chicken or egg.
Old snake,
you have one last chore.

Of all who have lived upon this land,
     alone,
I am cursed with eyes that cannot close.

John Wesley Stewert

You'd think a man might rest,
under six feet of dirt and sand,
his eyes dried like raisins,
ears consumed by worms,
his tongue silenced without the wind to utter
    words.
Fifty-nine years of struggling to draw
    breath,
he should lie in quiet, black solitude.

Oh, what I learned,
in the first millisecond of afterlife.
A man is but the child of a child of a child,
and his knowledge is not even that of
    a stone.
My eyes now number with the stars,
they see from the comet's tail

to the valley of shadows behind the moon.
My ears are now in tune with every
animal, fish, and bug from far Pluto
to the skin of the sun.
My voice is carried in the summer storm,
as in the whisper of the breeze,
and my knowledge is the school of God.

This night sky curves above me,
and in its arch I see reflected
every inch of this acreage
occupied by sleeping mortals,
the few remaining animals,
fields uncut and untilled
and under siege by hordes of greedy men.
I knew this time would come,
and though I weep rain clouds
and rage in the lightning bolt
and grumble in the throat of thunder,
I cannot escape the memory
of a man who cast his seed.
My fruit flourished and grew
above the dirt, unrooted,
my children not bound to land
that must yield the harvest by sickle,
better suited in this time to the bulldozer's
      blade.

Can I scorn them for becoming
exactly what I asked?

Across the slope of this hill
shines the night light in the great house
where my children sleep.
At the edge of the far wood,
Fenner's small house is aglow
like the moon rising,
and he does not sleep for he is possessed.
The bull is gone, the fields are cut
    with flags,
the fescue has seeded,
and Fenner knows his last chore he pledged
in oath.
That thought buzzes and torments him
like a swarm of one-million mosquitoes
alight a naked man.

A soul must right what he left undone
    as man
if he is then to rest
in a dark spot between two distant stars.
Let me lift from these bones, God,
my eye shall be the firefly,
my tongue the ceaseless clock,
and I will speak to them in dreams.

My spirit floats on the night air.
Bear me to their beds.
I am the summer storm.

Strange to pass through walls
like smoke through screen wire,
nails I once hammered to contain my vision
     of the world.
Stranger yet to be back in a man's house
and know it is no longer home,
for he is now a resident of the universe.
Stranger still to gaze upon one's first-born,
Julia.
Even in her sleep her eyelids jerk,
and she curls like one hunted by the world.
Child, have I done such that even in your
     dreams
your life pulls and pushes you
like now I feel the ebb and tug of the moon?

Can a man love deeper than his first-born?
If I could I would draw from you every
     trouble
even if I must pay with time in hell.
What hell have I given you, first girl,

that you despise these fields and pastures
    and woods?
Was it keeper of the innocent one?
I asked much,
that a young woman be asked to raise her
    weak sister,
but I did not possess the teat, the patience
or the soft hands to hold and caress one so
    small.
I was not man enough when living to
    cull her
as I would have the imperfect lamb,
the young rabbits with mother sliced by
    mower blades.
I did not praise enough your nightly
    lullabies
or compliment clean sheets and good meals.
Always my mind dwelled on the unplanted
    field,
the crop soon to bear.

Do not think, Julia, I did not know,
or care.
The young men who called
until they grew tired of refusals.
I heard your words to them grow cold
as Orion's season.

The magazines the postman brought
of far lands and unfamiliar faces
I left untouched for you to gather, read,
    and stack
beneath your bed
the same as I filled the barn with bales
    of hay
to hide my whiskey.
Do not think I do not remember how your
    songs
once reminded me of rainfall,
and petered out to the silence of snowfall.

You might call me liar,
rise and slap me and curse my face
if I were still of bone.
But I have given you a gift, Julia,
that is surer than love,
the callous of not needing to love.
Do you remember my hands?
They once were covered with thick skin
that came from shucking corn, castrating
    hogs,
stretching barbed wire and holding to a life
that spun and twisted and turned back
    on me.

My heart was just as scorched and scarred
    and raw.
A man who loves a piece of earth
dies with every weed.
Let him see his first-child born crying and
    wet with blood
and from that day forth he wants to bathe
    and clothe her.
Let one be born as simple as the flower,
and he blames his own seed.
Let him bury his wife,
and he knows why God made tears.

Julia,
if I have spared you a full heart
you are better,
for every second we love
we are held in bondage
for the remainder of our years.
Can you not go now to your magazine
    visions,
drink the good wine, bed the fishermen,
dance and dine like one possessed
not by land and love,
but only life?
A heart of steel does not tarnish or crack
    or bleed.

In your absence,
the dust of my bones will nourish your
    empire
of flowers and they will grow tall and wild
as your dreams
and wave like flags to guide you home
    one day.
You can call the tulip your daughter;
the holly bush will be your son,
and if he or she should not grow with a
    perfect stem and petal,
pluck it and bury another bulb.

You will not weep for flowers.

David,
you sleep more soundly than your sister.
Does your mind lay more in peace
or do you shut the world on and off
like closing the cover on one of your books?
If I had hands and were a vengeful soul,
I might close the whispering wind from
    your nostrils
and declare you a traitor-son,
one who sells his father's hard-wrought
    land.

From my bed, I have watched the surveyor
    crews
cut this fine acreage from oak forest to
    river bank,
their ribbons the flags of a generation that
    surrendered
from a life coaxed and plucked from
    the land.
I wept grains of sand when the bull was led
    away,
the favored sow whose ears I scratched,
a farm forged through sweat and blood,
whittled to what few acres surround the
    great house,
the hill of grave stones,
and Lola's water rocks.

I hold no vengeance,
for you are only the man I molded,
the fruit of a seed planted and fertilized
with my own juices.
My torment is only equaled by my pride.
What books do I know?
The Bible, *Huckleberry Finn*, and
    The Farmer's Almanac.
My education was in sunburn and chapped
    hands.

For every ear of fat corn I have husked,
I have seen another shrivel
or gnawed by worms.
Boy,
your world is rapidly changing,
and no longer can a man live easy
off the fruit of his land.

What grain and fruits I have watched sprout
and flourish under God's sun,
will one day grow as well or better in
    greenhouses,
without need of clear skies and plows.
It is good that my child and his child
won't dirty their hands, bleed and sweat,
when their labor can be welded from within
    their mind,
and thought and tongue replace the
    hard-flexed muscle.
I have pushed you from this land,
as surely as the robin nudges the young bird
from the home bough,
and my price has been paid, as with you,
in too many good-byes,
handshakes instead of hugs,
and a son who does not share my love
    of earth.

Is it better?
I am convinced,
as I wish I could say
to you and your sister,
that a full heart is man's great weakness,
and fares as fragile as a Mason jar
filled with honey and dashed against rocks.
Books will not deceive you,
or fail you in dry season or hailstorm,
and while my tongue has both praised
and cursed the seasons,
may yours only speak of what is known
    and tried.
May they call you teacher,
and your harvest lie in words.

Sleep, boy, without dreams or fear of failure.
I have not cultivated a finer stalk of corn,
nor seen wheat so ripe and bursting as you.
What I have lost in loosening you from
    the land,
might you one day deliver to your offspring.
Maybe the time not spent worrying over
    seed corn,
and the laboring sow,
can be traded back in unencumbered love.
If I failed you, failed Julia,

my fault lay only in a heart as cracked and
    fissured
as a field without rain.

Lola,
sleep your rest of angels,
for you alone, child, live without the fear,
anguish or guilt.
Dream girl, barefoot one,
to my lips and heart you were the one
who brought cool water.
What is it in a God who bears to Earth one
    like the lamb
that man calls simple?

In my life child,
I saw in your lustrous skin
all that I wish life could be,
a people who believe first without reason
    to doubt.
In you I could love without excuses.
If the perch flipped off your fishing line,
I could explain it was only so,
and not the fault of the hook or line
or how you held the pole.
If you asked me why the sky was blue,
I felt no shame in saying I did not know.

You would nod and say maybe
that was God's favorite color.
Your hand in my palm
was warm with the blood of my own,
and I did not feel the tension of differing sex
that stays the embrace of even father and
    daughter.

I am dust now,
one with the atoms, and have no arms to
    entwine you
and blanket you from a world that demands
    facts.
And child,
what I had feared in my life dreams,
and saw slowly grow like mold,
in the eyes of your brother and sister,
I now see manifest in land cut and
    measured,
divided and drawn
without fields and oak stands
for barefoot wandering woman-girls.

Lola,
had I been the timekeeper of my last hour,
I would have set you free to explore and
    question

a universe that knows no surveyor lines or
    boundaries,
safe from the binding girds
of heartbeat and breathing.
Look into the deep river water and see my
    reflection.
It shimmers and turns with the wind,
the flip of minnow fins.
Follow me into the land without walls.

I can leave this house now.
I have spoken, and what excuses offered
come from a grave hardened with lament.
Across the field
Fenner's light still burns,
and he waits.
His hammer I have listened to these weeks
as he labored to mend fences
trampled down as paper walls
before Gideon's trumpet.
He swung that bell as his own voice and
    pleaded
against time and change.
We are the dinosaurs, old buddy,
the aged boxer downed in the ring.
I will ask you one last favor,
and then we shall be set free.

Whiskey, Fenner?
Many times we shared the same bottle.
I see by the dim light
you shared this one with no man.
Your face mashed against the table,
the wind whistles in your nose like troubled
	birds.
This whiskey sleep you have earned;
you have earned much.

The time is right, Fenner,
or the time so wrong
it can never be made right again.
Our world is not their world.
The corn is shriveled, the weeds tall,
and the nestling hare is left without a
	guardian.
I have spoken to her, and she will
	follow you
to the rocks, and the quiet sheen of the
	deep pool.
A door opens there into a brighter land.

Part Five

Fenner

Wake up, child, but hush now.
Your brother and sister still sleep,
but I have promised too long to take you
to the river. Your eyes are large, listen.
The rocks spoke to me in my dreams,
and told me we shall take our breakfast
from the perch and bream.
We shall drench our eyes,
and in the morning sun see rainbows.
Hurry now.
Wrap in your shawl,
for the morning is young and cool fog hugs
    the field.
Crawl through this window very quietly,
for David and Julia are still weary,
and we shall surprise them with our
    gillstring of fishes.

Is the dew cold?
I should have laced you in your sneakers.
No, we are not forgetting the cane pole,
the can of worms.
We will catch these fish in our hands.
Come quickly, the sun burns,
and we are not two sleepy heads,
unlike the lazy rooster who has yet
to crow this morning.
The rocks have spoken to me
and told me secrets.
You can hear their whisper
where the clouds and sun lie upon the water.

Julia

What is this night that torments me?
I have dreamed of great winds, fire
        and storms.
My father standing by my bedside, his arms
        outstretched
and drenched with blood.
And now the sun is blood-red and hangs
in the forest like the eye
of a weary, angered God.
My heart beats fast and loud in my ear.

This house breathes.
My window shade draws and bumps against
        the pane,
and my bedroom door closes inch by inch.
I hear the tinkle of the Chinese wind charm.
Perhaps Lola looks out her window

to the graveyard while she waits
for his return.
I should rise, and bundle her back in bed
and explain with a hug that he will visit her
	best
in her dreams.
For one who knows no guilt or shame,
his arms will drip with honey.

An open window?
Where have you gone, Lola?
To feed the chicks in the barn?
I have told you the hen pecks.
Shake it off, woman.
Nightmares haunt not only children.
Your father still sleeps his eternal rest
on the hillside, and your sister
feeds cracked corn to chickens,
and this life continues to move day to day,
and page to page.
Fetch her.

This barn door sings in a shrill pitch of
	mourning.
Has old Fenner forgotten what grease is for?
Lola, answer me;
are you hiding in the empty hay loft,

or behind the old enameled bath tub
where the stud bull slaked his rutting thirst?
I am not angry
at one whose dawn desire
is to feed the old rooster,
his frowsy hens and peeping, yellow chicks.

I hear no yard fowl scratching the dry dust
of their nesting pen,
no Lola's hushed giggle from a stall or
    corner
of this dusty building.
The rooster I have so cursed on early
    mornings
is silent this day.
Is he sleeping,
his rest also stalled by the dream of storms?

Great God in Heaven!
In the dirt at my feet lies a great snake,
his belly as taunt and round as a melon.
His mouth leaks the yellow of eggs,
and the chicken yard is littered with feathers
    and carnage—
seven dead hens, the rooster
still bound in loops of the snake's coils,

his fighting spur buried deep inside the
    serpent's eye.
Do I still dream, my nightmare returned?
Lola,
answer me!

David

I dreamed I was drowning,
swimming upwards from a deep, deep pool,
my lungs bursting as I kicked and pulled
toward the bright, sunlit surface.
Finally, with my chest consumed by flames
my head emerged
and I spewed dead air and drew great lungs
full of the living breath.

Three heavy breaths I drew,
of cool, sweet, morning air
before I realized I was safe in my bed.
But such are dreams,
the terror of imagined death tempered
by reawakening to the world.
This morning is very quiet.
Julia and Lola are still sleeping;

the old rooster must be resting
between his fits of crowing.
Even old Fenner sits late.
He has worn his hammer to a nub,
but he seems at last to realize
that the labor of his past
now allows him to sip
his second cup of coffee
while the sun dries the dew-drenched fields.

Later the noise will begin.
The trucks and graders will come,
furrowing the earth in contours
for a new crop.
I have decided to leave three acres fallow
surrounding the graveyard
where mother and father rest.
I will plant shrubs
and build wooden benches, maybe a
        fish pool
and a sign will proclaim "Stewert Park,"
a tribute to a passing life and age.
Maybe there among the bramble
of blackberry bushes and wisteria vines
the old rat snake I have seen these many
        years
can find refuge for his remaining time

and song birds will nest in the oak branches
above where my parents lie.

But, that is work for tomorrow.
In this minute my lungs are full
and the sun still low
and my eyes feel the call
of sweet, untroubled sleep.

Fenner

Child,
listen to me, and I will tell you a story
while you dangle your toes in the water.
It is of your father and fishes,
the union of man, air and water,
and of why we have trees, clouds and soil.
Did you really think your father was
        sleeping
on the hilltop in the gray box,
covered with earth and flowers.
He was never one to rest that way—we lied.
He has become a part of the wind and
        the sky,
of the moon and water.
See him there in the stream?
Look deep, child.
His face is reflected,

eyes blue as the sky, his graying hair
the rain cloud.
Trace his wrinkles with your fingertips,
those laugh lines and crow's feet
ripple the water as he smiles
and waits for you.
Remember his gold tooth?
See it sparkling there in the sun's reflection.
He whispers to you in the robin's song.
Listen.

"Come to me, Lola,
and I will hug you in arms
that wrap like warm bath water
and ease you through a door
where we will know no walls or boundaries
or be separated anymore."

Julia

I will talk sharp to Fenner,
for today he has acted as silly as Lola.
Their tracks lead
down the sand path toward the river.
If I had known he planned to take her
    fishing
I would still be buried beneath my covers.
She is barefoot,
her tender heel and toe prints
like a fawn walking beside Fenner
in his hob-nailed brogans.
I will fuss at him. This sand is cold.
It's strange he would take her so early,
without breakfast or shoes.
But no stranger than this morning,
with the sun so rcd

and already clouds on the horizon that rear
    dark heads.
That rat snake bursting with eggs.
Did he really believe he could kill and
    swallow
the feisty rooster?

From this high bank the river shines
like a knife blade,
and I see Fenner.
He sits at midstream upon a rock.
Do I hear some strange bird?
Lola, where are you child?
I am tired of games.
Fenner, are you weeping,
or do you shake with laughter
at the child's hide and seek?
You tremble and your chest heaves long
    and slow
like a weary man.
What do you watch in the water?
It is deep
and blue
and white
as a portrait of the sky.

Lola

I do see you, Daddy.
Your eyes and wrinkles and gold tooth.
I did not know
you could talk like birds
and breathe the same as fishes.

Mr. Fenner says today is my real birthday,
and we will feast on peach ice cream,
that you have for me a surprise
so large I cannot hold it in both hands.
The river gets deeper with every step
but Fenner says you will teach me to breathe
    like the bream,
and give me wings to fly like the robin.

Daddy, hold me,

like you used to carry me home when I was
    sleepy.
Peach ice cream is cold and the sun is warm
and I am ready to learn to fly.

Books by Tim McLaurin

The Acorn Plan
Woodrow's Trumpet
Keeper of the Moon: A Southern Boyhood
Cured by Fire
The Last Great Snake Show
Lola

1/98

GAYLORD S